# Controlled Khaos



Krash Mat

BookLeaf
Publishing

Presentation by *BookLeaf Publishing*

Web: www.bookleafpub.com

E-mail: info@bookleafpub.com

ISBN: 978-93-5744-834-5

First edition 2022

# DEDICATION

This book is dedicated to every individual who has crossed my path and made an impact on my life. I wrote this book because you all helped shape me into the many forms and versions of myself I've loathed and learned to love. The experiences inspired me to share my gift and voice. I am humbled and grateful.

“We don't meet people by accident. They are meant to cross our paths for a reason.”
–Unknown.

A True and Sincere, Thank You.

# ACKNOWLEDGEMENT

A heartfelt thank you to BookLeaf Publishing, My Soul Tribe, My fiancé, and the experiences of life!

# PREFACE

This is a personal and poetic think piece, and collection of thoughts, feelings, and emotions come to varying points of dissection, reflection, and fruition. A very personal introduction to Krash Mat, this book is an exploration through poetic perspective of her interpretations of self, and levels of self-awareness amongst different points and times, situations, and mindsets throughout her life; which was the inspiration for her firstwork.

# The Start [Realizing My Capabilities]

Higher state of mind

I feel it's almost time

I'm right there at the door

The other side is more

Blessed abundance be,

It's right in front of me,

I have to be patient,

But I'll never be complacent

I am not contended

Doesn't mean ungrateful

I want break my ceiling

I know God is willing

I mean that from my soul

Because God ONLY knows

And I pray about it,

Got this gift and my dream,

Puzzle pieced it together,

Flowing through a conscious stream

I want the world to see

I want the world to feel

My contribution to the mission of helping the world heal

Breaking barriers, and touching hearts

More to come in the future, but right here is The Start.

# Unpacked [An Awakening]

I've been surrounding myself in positivity,
trying to live life intently.
Be fully present in my existence.

Approaching, what used to seem impossible,
valiantly and standing on my own two feet more
firmly planted.

The inner voices say they're proud of me, and
unlike myself, have never doubted me, and I
come to myself more gently now, because after
years of survival I'm living now.

Taking into account the things I've been through
and learned,
like understanding what a protective gift it is to
discern;
and what this gift has given me, and what a
guide it's been to me.

I'm an introspective introvert, and I'm always
listening and observing things.

I've come to respect those things about myself, and I'm learning to live with my mistakes.

A rising Phoenix, born again, more knowledge and logic from the toils of life.

Slowly but with conviction, unfolding myself like a flower in bloom.
Respecting my ongoing journey and the timing of it too.

Letting go of guilt, no more locking myself away.

No longer putting everyone else and their thoughts and feelings ahead of me.

I've been forging my own path,

trying to keep my vibrations high, and to say that I don't get tired or struggle, would be a useless little lie.

Each day is a gift, and my stats are the same, I've made it through 100% of even my worst days.

I keep myself more present, and better mentally prepared.

Fully speaking my truth.

Fully seeking myself.

Being honest about what I need.

Being honest with myself.

Saying sorry when it's hard.

When things are hard, finally saying enough.

I've been in my spiritual closet, unpacking so much stuff.

Keeping things that fit, and what doesn't, throwing it away.

Just because it fit a year ago, does not mean it will today.

I have gained the understanding that I plan to never be too content.
To keep reaching and striving, for I am sure, I'm meant for more.

Having so much to give.

This is now how I live.

Unpacked.

# A Trip Down My Rabbit Hole [Who I Was]

It took some time for me to see, verily
The version and vision of myself I've come to be
For so long I had been hidden
Sheathed
Covered in a veil so convincing, you could not fathom an underneath

I was reflective fragments of who I thought others wanted and needed me to be
Parts of them, they wished to see in me
I people pleased
And for some time,
It pleased me back

Until the cost of this way of living, I could no longer pay back
I felt attacked
By my own psyche
To me, it screamed,
THIS IS HOW IT'S SUPPOSED TO BE!

If that were true, then why to my detriment, was
I feeling so dis-eased?

I did not feel like my life was my own property
I felt I owed everyone what was to become of
me
The sum of me, but I also needed some of me
I know now in reality, I was compensating for a
lacking inside me
My inner child ruling my psychology, trying to
figure out a way to get what she needs

But, nobody had known, they could not perceive
I painted so pretty a picture, that it was all that
was seen
But then there was me
A little girl trapped in a corner crying, and
hugging her knees
She was me, and for so long I feigned content
But inside was hellbent on a way to quit

But then what would my purpose be?
If I truly felt I belonged to me?
My worth seemed so much to revolve around, A
self-destructive selflessness
But there was an exigency to evolve somehow
My safe and reliable way of living, became
something worth resolving now...

# Things I Try To Remember [Consciousness & Self-Awareness]

Quiet down your ego

Your soul is regal

Love is light

Life is difficult

Self-care can simply be respite

We are infinite

This life is finite

Live your truths

Make yourself the living proof

Find yourself in the grey sometimes

Black & White aren't all that exist

Fear is fuel

Doing it afraid makes you brave

Can you know true pleasure without pain?

Sometimes, dance in the rain

Just be

And become

Find your peace

Manifest your blessings to be

Be self aware

Only you can create your own reality

# What Would You Do? [Reflecting & Dissecting] (Early Days)

I didn't think that you'd believe me

If I'd spoken to you the truth.

"What happens in this house, stays in this house!"

Is what I was told as a youth.

It sat

deep

down

within me,

like a shadow of my burden as a child;

It was in that phrase I vowed to hide those things with a masked smile.

Keep it all in,

they'll never know.

Though I longed and pained to tell you so;

Things said to me,

and life unfair,

the things that I experienced there.

I was so lonely,

in comfort confined,

to pity and self sabotage of my young developing mind,

It wasn't all bad, but it wasn't all good, and I thought if I said anything, it'd bring more trouble and I'd be misunderstood.

Who would I tell?

What would I say?

Not a finger was ever laid to me.

I'm sensitive and being soft, can't take some words?

Is that really all?

Strive for perfection, that not even they could achieve.

Homework, cook and clean.

Duties of the oldest 3.

Make sure this house is spic and span, everyday that was my plan.

Siblings need help with homework?

I give them a hand, term myself a second mother in my youth.

Dinner for my siblings, bathe them, then bed.

Get myself together too.

I often wondered, “If like me you’re not working, who’s the parent?”

Me or you?

I’m sure you may think what others thought too.

"You’re an older sibling, that’s what you’re supposed to do."

Not when a parent capable of the tasks did nothing but sleep and sit on their ass.

The other worked all through the day, and came home late, no time to play.

That was my life, day in and out.

Take care of everyone, parents scream and shout.

At each other,

And at us,

back and forth they always fussed.

Mostly didn’t feel I could do right, even tried breaking up a fight.

Home life didn't always feel safe, but there was always food on my plate.

And I continued to smile, pretending fine all the while.

Learning things I thought to be right.

If only life could be so simple, if only things were black and white.

But reality is areas of grey, I learned so much of what I saw and experienced was not okay.

I wanted to tell, but who would believe the story I just told, and if they did what would've happened to me?

What would have happened to my family?

Would my parents be mad?

Doing all I could to be good, they'd for sure think me bad.

Back to that phrase in my youth, I held those words for truth.

If you'd been in my situation, what would you do?

# Blank [Heavy Introspection]

I had 2 pictures of us
1 I kept, the other I ripped to shreds
It portrays us happy
Daughter and Father
That moment was during a different time, when my grandmother was still alive
I was less than the age of 5
I recall no memory of the moment, only what was captured
I never asked who took the photo
I assumed my mother
Now I wonder

I found out yesterday that you may not have so much time left on this side of
the fence
I feel bad, but some stoic part of me won't allow me to feel sad
I feel, like I don't feel
Growing up, I had questions that time and experience helped to heal
I had false hope for us

I guess, I blamed myself for you not being around
Maybe I'm not good enough, why doesn't he want me?
Why doesn't he love me?

I got kind of lost in the imaginary personality I created of you
My father loves me, one day he'll come for me, he misses me
And time went on
You were more a rolling stone to me
I never got to have you
Not in the ways I needed to

At some point in time
For me, you just existed
In strange memories on the occasional birthday
My mother allowed you into the home she'd made for me
You may have brought me a gift, given me some money, and then you cried
I remember that
You often cried when I'd see you
It didn't make sense to me
But now I'm wondering if I felt some sense of responsibility to your feelings inadvertently?

Also, sometimes you'd call.
Tell me you were on the way.
Say that we could get ice cream or go to the park
I waited for you until it got dark
No call, no show
Too many times
If being my father was a job, you'd have
undoubtedly been fired

My memories of you are few
A couple birthdays, after the party was over,
moments of time, maybe a holiday
A cheek swab to see if we shared the same DNA
And sporadic as it was
Nothing more to truly say

I reached out on my own when I was grown
I tried for myself to find the reasons why
Although the damage to my heart was done, the
peace I thought I'd get was unattainable in any
answers from you, which again were few
I stopped blaming you for my heartache, and
stopped shaming me for my feelings of
inadequacy attached to feeling like an unloved,
unwanted child

I still want to talk about that shame though
In your nonappearance in my life, I learned that
my siblings born of you

felt the same, even though they got more time
I felt some kind of way, being first in line and getting the smallest portion of love, fathering, and time
Saw you in photographs with them growing up
Resentment bubbled up
But I don't dislike you
I don't hate you

I feel grateful to have been born into this life
Thankful you were not there
I learned invaluable lessons and couldn't be who I am today, If you were part of things
My mom and my dad raised me right
Did all they could with everything they had
I turned out more than okay, or alright

I thrive

At this very moment in time, I'm wondering if you're still alive
Maybe I'll feel for you at a different time
This experience is somewhat of a fear of mine
What and if I'd feel for you at this time
Tupac lines comes to mind,

'He passed away and I didn't cry, 'cause my anger
Wouldn't let me feel for a stranger'

I related
I'm not elated
I'm not even in pain
It's more an unemotional strain
An analysis of my memories of you
Trying to feel something for you, maybe I do:

Blank

# Free [My Interpretation]

No lock • No key • No cage

No fear

No guarded emotions to mend over the years

Vulnerability • Possibilities

Absolution & Tranquility

Willingness

to share my gift

Glowing and full hearted,

Doing as I wish

Seeing fit

To live,

A life worth living

Give

love

worth giving

Breathe

Eat meals unhurried

•Be•

Unbothered & unworried

•Be•

~•~Free~•~

# How did it Happen? [More Reflection]

You wish for me to climb mountains knowing
I'm inept.

Did you want me to prove something to you?

See how far I'd go?

Push and pull myself along at your request
because you just want me to do it?

Bloody my hands on jagged ridges, leave myself
without a life line, no support.

Did you expect I'd come back?

Or did you want to see me fail in my attempt to
please your ego?

Give you a reason to scold me for not achieving
yet another marking point on the scale of
contention.

You're always right, especially when you're wrong.

And I'm always wrong, even when I've demonstrated all that you've asked, some things you did not.

You give me nothing but broken hope that you may change, no matter that you continue to stay the same.

I'm never enough, and empty, I still try pouring into your cup and it's full.

Why do we continue this dance?

I beg you to let me off this carousel, but it's your amusement park.

You complain of its shabbiness, but make no effort to fix it up or upgrade.

You like it as it is, as long as I'm your clown, equipped with a painted smile.

Outside appearance is all you really care about.

You don't want anyone to come in, just want to present the facade.

Let me know that you'd give tickets out for free if I were to leave, but you'd never let me.

You find far too much comfort in my slow demise, at your hand, controlling the depths of every breath in and out.

I've died countless times, and come back, upon resuscitation because you do not wish me peace.

You think me a pet on a leash.

Give me treats when I'm "good."

When I "stay."

You beat me, place me in a cage when you're displeased,

all the while telling me I could be, "free if you wanted."

Oh the frailty of my mind, my dignity.

I left my self-worth somewhere, long ago to lighten the load for who you'd have me be.

Is this on me?

# Good-Bye [A Lifted Weight/A Key Unwillingly Given]

Why did you look at me that way?

As if you were going to say,

That I'd hurt you.

After everything you put me through, and pushed me through, and the ways you made us both punish me for your shortcomings and wrong doings.

I didn't know I had a problem. That I was addicted to your behavior pattern, because it mimicked my experience of growing up.

I didn't know that I was ill prepared for love.

I didn't know that I hadn't the foggiest of notions about what love was.

When you haven't seen it, and it hasn't been correctly given, the lesson of love becomes an oxymoron like false truth.

I didn't know I would deny

myself

my own rights of emotion

While I supplied you with support and devotion.

I had no boundaries because I thought that love was supposed to be unconditional.

For me, that message was traditional.

You beat me with your words.

You put me in my place, and I thought part of love was to obey and in my place I stayed.

I cried for myself in secret, kept up appearances, lied to survive.

I lied to people I loved, and myself, some days I felt like I'd die.

I only noticed my deterioration of health when I could no longer ignore it.

Swore that, If only I were prettier the way you liked, did it that way, rid myself of the things in me you despised,

Then your real true love I could comprise.

I lived with the death of myself.

For you.

Not knowing at the time the true depths of *my* soul.

It was not until you tip toed too far over the line, that I

could wrap around my mind, the concept of this time genuinely being the last time.

That I

Would no longer grin and bear it.

I was learning to love myself and reclaim my self esteem, and not to deem myself unworthy, for the things I didn't know, and to also take responsibility for my part in the reruns of this tired show.

There was an opportunity out, and this time I was able to go.

You tried everything within your power.

All the tactics that worked before.

To keep me still believing in you and from walking out the door but I said, “No more.”

And those eyes,

The silence, and that was after pleading and rage, you looked at me almost empty, a dog with its tail between its legs.

You looked at me that way, but I opened the door to your surprise, I looked at you right back, and before the door closed, I said, “Good-Bye.”

# Almost/Finally [Epiphany/Awakening]

I couldn't quite say I knew how to feel free.
I know it started with no longer being anchored to a slowly sinking ship;
Pain, taking off my rose colored blinders, and taking accountability.
Some of the answers were within who I wanted to become,
Others from without who I thought at that time that I was;
And framed, by lessons learned in a nearly imminent drowning...

I needed to search myself, read the book of me.
Maybe I missed some things?
I travelled down, up, and floated; trying incessantly, fervently to break through.
And I began to wake up.
I was on a journey to a version of me I had yet to be,

Desiring to know all of myself and find the lost pieces along the way.

I wanted peace and clarity.
I began to unearth treasures not lost, but buried to me.
I summoned myself, became more self-aware, began to practice self care,
I meditated and drank in nature in a way I cannot say I had ever appreciated before.

God truly existed in my space, and from that moment on never left from me.
I was reintroduced to my light,
My truths, willpower, and might.
My mind, would never be the same.
It was as if I'd undergone some rewiring of my brain.

I realized that there would be people who'd questioned my sanity,
The God in me and my use of profanity.
I also realized what I did and who I was, was only the business of me.
So mind your business if you catch me talking to the trees, singing through the breeze, dancing under the moon, or in sunlight.

I was free!

That's it!
That's all.
That's me!

Finally, feeling free.

# Ascending [Awakening/Desire]

I was caught in the unconscious collective
stream of a listless sleepwalking scene.
Melancholy haunted me, like misery loves
company.
But I fell in line just fine, I wasn't the only one
to eat, work, sleep, repeat.
I'd moan out complaints of things being the
same with no actions toward change, and so, the
cycle was complete.

At some point upon recommencing,
I became more self-aware, introduced me, to me
amongst truths of what I could be.
The 9 to 5 grind started feeling unaligned, and
stopped fulfilling me.
I suddenly felt stifled and uneased, displeased
with what was put in front of me.
I would not eat.
I craved true sustenance that my way of living at
the time could not feed.

Hunger grew within me, and it was a feeling I had to feed.
That is when a great indifference set in for me.
To remain the same was leaving me empty and drained.
I continuously applied change, relentlessly attempting to give myself the reality I craved and break from the collective of the dream-dead enslaved.

This was not that path for me that was paved.
My ancestors love, light, and trauma flowing through my soul from beyond the grave.
They did what they did, gave what they gave so that someone next in the lineage could resolve the mistakes they made.
So their trauma and abuses were not in vain, someone needed to be brave.
Break the cycles that have been but did not need to be maintained, so their souls would no longer be chained to the same pains and shame.

They and I are the same.
Blessing bestowed upon me in my glory, telling my, and their story. The power of so many lives completed, living inside of me.

Once again, now more awake, nothing I've been through in my life was a mistake.

Where I should be, no matter the mystery
beyond where my steps will take me, and
nothing can shake me.

Ascending.

# Beating The Beasts [An Expression]

Depression & Anxiety
Raging beasts living inside of me
Gnawing teeth penetrating me violently
Outwardly attacking me quietly
They exhausted me undeniably
Redefined the progressions of who I was trying to be
Caffeine in the mornings seemed unescapable
Diphenhydramine in the evenings so sleep was capable
Neither soothe the beasts, as they devoured me
I shivered under my covers feeling cowardly
With them around, the mask was more important now
I felt in need of mental hallowed ground
No one ever really asked if I was okay
The mask I wore, virtually always on display
Even at my worst I could still pretend, until I was home again and I could purge what I'd been holding in
I cried for hours, couldn't clean, wouldn't shower

These beasts inside never contented with their power
What small semblance of control I had was slipping loose,
I felt physical pain, and to no one much use
Would there be anything to miss if I didn't exist?
My thoughts spiraled on and on like this
Hope for a future, for which I truly had to fight
was the only thing that stopped me from not waking up one night
Though sometimes these beasts still bother me,
Thankfully they're mostly tamed and no longer my plight
Suited now in mental body armor, I'm up for the challenge and prepared to fight

Amen

# Chang[ing] [Release of Fear/More Introspection]

I am unashamed and imperfect

I sit and talk with my demons on a daily basis

I'm trying to understand my shadow

I want to know who I am,

so I can become fully who I want to be

It's okay if you don't wish to sit next to me

My energy can be overwhelming

Sometimes I'm

swallowed

by my emotions

They get the best of me

But each day,

I begin

again

Learning

how to become my own best friend

Integrating

healthy voices inside of my head

I'm only as great

as the best

version of me

Starting with

'the man in the mirror'

I started to see

myself clearer

And everything that

follows me,

Haunts me,

Taunts me,

But it's all me

And now the idea of change,

That for me held so much fear,

Even some shame,

Calms me

Because I know I don't have to be the same

# Boundaries [Exploration & Dissection]

I did not know I could build walls.
It was hard for me, because the only walls I could see seemed to be the walls around me.
Walls surround me, limiting my exploration, but not the expectations to which I had always upheld.

I did not know, I could build walls.
It was not that I didn't do it, it was that there was no option for it at all.
How I would have loved to demand, no trespassing!
Herein lies myself, and my time, and YOU MAY NOT, disturb my peace or disrupt my thoughts.
This is where I draw my line.
This is me, with a made up mind.

I did not know I needed walls.
But without walls, I was a free for all.

Discomfort was not a new feeling at all,
So I complied, even though my agreeance was a lie, and I was less than enthralled.

I needed walls.
I needed them to build and heal, though I did not know it needed to be learned.
I didn't know putting boundaries in place was a skill.
For so long, I hadn't had a voice.
I didn't know I had a choice, but today as I live and breathe,
You'll have to respect my boundaries if you want to deal with me.

# Land Here [What I Have To Give]

Krash into my words, and land softly on my
Mat.
Tell me where your head and heart are at?
I offer healing in the form of this gift,
the dripping brown sugar from the peak of my
pen.
You need not feel forlorn.
We must all go through storms.
We could not appreciate light, if at first we
hadn't experienced night.
Pain, a blessing sometimes in disguise. It may
hurt, but it's a sign you're alive.

Let me cradle you with my experience,
teach you lessons that may lessen your own
remiss.
Help you find and create your own bliss.
You were made for this!

We create our own reality by being self-aware,
Start listening to your own calling, by sounds
not heard by ear.

I hope to bring you to yourself, I've been placed
in your path to be of help.
Remember that knowledge is true wealth, but
not only things you find in books,
Sometimes introspection is key to where we
must look.

Know that help is all around, our ancestors do
hear your cries, trust your intuition and let your
spirits guide.

# Dear Little Me [Poem to Self]

Dear Little Me,

My God, I love you so. Here are some things that I think you should know: You're not for everybody and not meant to be 'gotten', you are special and perfectly you little brown Goddess! Keep working and striving and chasing your dream, it will never be as far off as you think it may seem. If ever you feel alone, know God and your guides are always protecting you and by your side. Don't let what others want for you become your only choice, take that road less travelled by, speak up and use your voice. Keep spreading love and positivity. It really is helping others, though you can't always see. Your parents do the best they can, with everything they have at hand, and your brothers truly are built in best friends. Love who you'd like, and not be default. Don't give up on yourself at any cost. Love vulnerably but with boundaries in place. Live and know it's okay to take up space. Things you think inside of you have been killed, will come back after time to heal, and understanding at that time will seal the deal. You're important, you're enough, spend more time with and being honest with those you love.

Love,
The Future Version of Us

# Warrioress [Purpose/Power]

I was made to slay demons.
Especially my own.
A Warrioress that don't take no mess,
But my heart is not one of stone.
I feel, I heal, and sometimes
I'm broken.

But I was made for this,
Built, to deconstruct the system, arrest, and
conquer it.
Tell me that I can't,
I'll prove to MYSELF that I can.
What you think or believe of me, doesn't
interfere with my plans.

My I am, I can,
Brings oases to dry lands
My reality is what I think it, and if it isn't, then
I'll make it.

I was made to slay demons,
even if the demons are part of me,

if I can salvage the broken peace, then I can
integrate it into a part of me,
Set up boundaries, tell insecurities to move
along,
That’s my strength
10 toes down,
Both emotional and strong
I am, I can, you're either with me,
Or move along.

# The Brewing Of The Storm [Excitement/Fear/Vulnerability]

I keep pieces of her in my mental.

She is so sweet, and her spirit so big!

But so gentle.

There's something so loud in her silence; it called to me.

I heard it speak, but;

I was not acquainted with the language.

I heard something so familiar, and unexplored,

A small, unexpected spark in me

Wanted to know more.

But; more of what?

I started, unknowingly collecting mental
snapshots of the brownness of her skin,
wondered the exact color of her eyes,

So I could commit that too

To my memory film.

The reel in my mind on only play and rewind.

What had gotten into me?

Come to find out it was she,

And she could also see me;

And here I was,

Thinking I somehow inconvenienced her with
my presence;

When in essence;

I found that I was a nuisance.

But, only because, all of that time,

I had taken up residence inside of her mind.

But my knowledge of that,

came later on,

This was the brewing of the storm.

# Because of Her [All In/In Love]

She is the equivalent of my desires

My soul parallel

- My Twin Flame-

Key element of my ascension

To know her is to know myself

To love her is to love myself

Her heart is patient with mine

~Love has never felt so divine~

<3

I mean God sent

Exactly what I need

She evoked in me a desire to heal

An aspiration to be more

With her I know who I want to be

With the words, "I love you, too" spoken,

Chains on my heart

Were broken

And I could love

Whole heartedly

Fully

Ripe

Hopefully

Joyfully

Blissfully

All because of

Her

# Poetic Guide [Inspiration/Fuel]

There were 2 paths that I could take.
I chose the road less travelled by,
I know that this was no mistake,
As no fate can keep us from the chosen way.
I could not live with,
It might have been, had not or that, or this.
I chose my path with what it'd bring, all
associated risks.

Challenging as this path might be,
I walk it daily, a step at a time.
I cannot say I've never strayed, or felt as though
I'd fallen behind;
But I am a woman phenomenally,
Even when I fall down, Still I Rise,
Knowing why the caged bird sings,
I sing my own melodies longing to be free.

I look down this path as far as I can see,
I'm not quite sure what's waiting afar,
but maybe if I can keep up my stride valiantly,

Then ages hence,
This could be your guide.

# Junk Drawer [My Mental/Emotional Energy]

I am full of things you can easily find, things there are no place for, and things we try to hide.
Sometimes,
I am stuffed to capacity,
and then I'm overloaded with more.
Things sometimes spill out of me, and end up lost or on the floor.

Occasionally I am rummaged through, if there's something you expect to find, but mostly while I'm existing, I'm also hidden in plain sight.
I hold batteries and bandages, thumbtacks and old paperclips.
Takeout menus old and new, expired coupons in here too.

And if you should search for things hard to find, you might just take something of mine, but I am always here to share, and bring you back to what you've lost.

For nothing is ever really gone, we either find it or just move on.

www.ingramcontent.com/pod-product-compliance
Lightning Source LLC
Chambersburg PA
CBHW051735130826
49812CB00033B/874
*9789357448345*